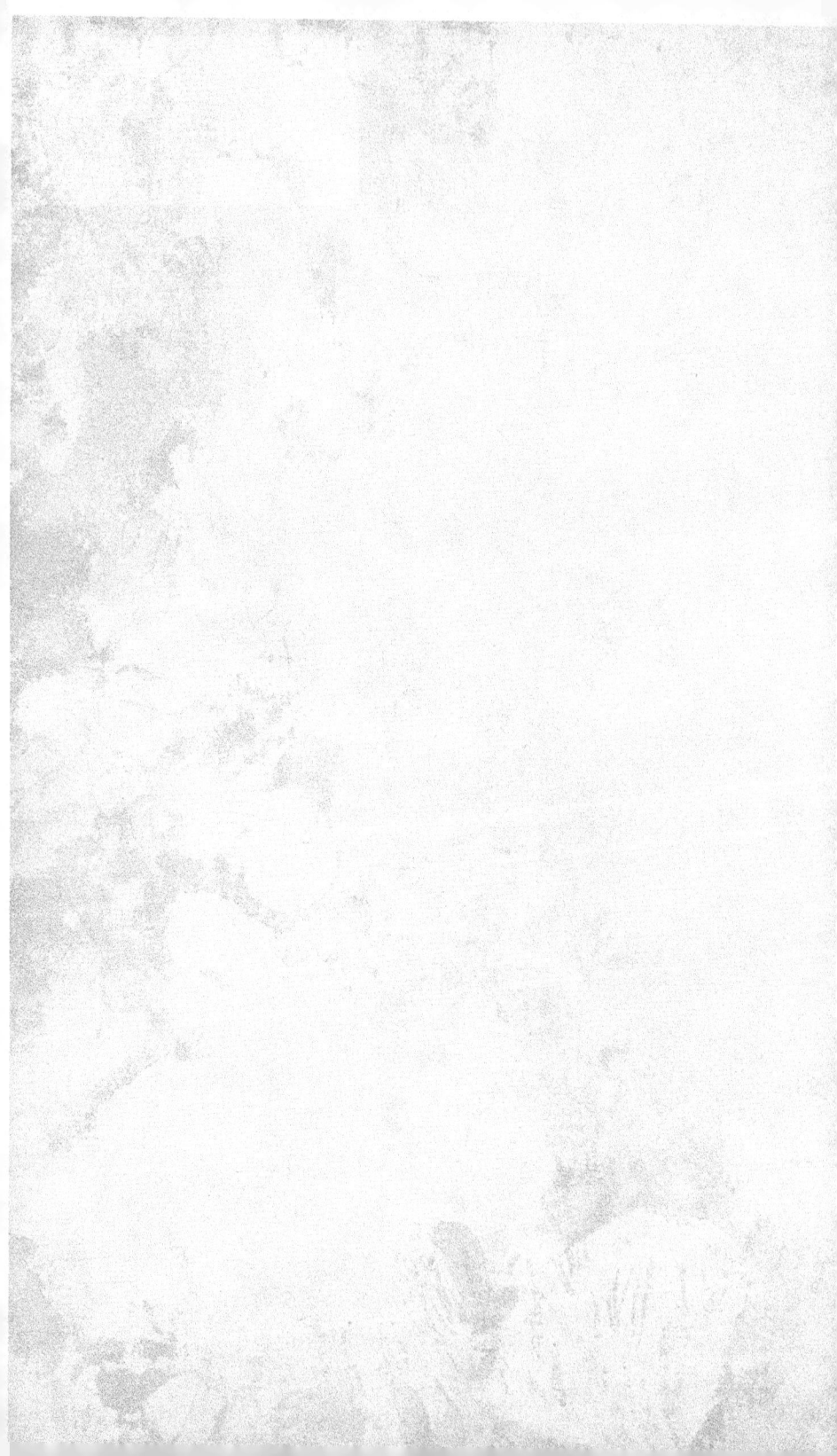

A Halo Publishing International Anthology

BECAUSE
LOVE
REMAINS

Stories of Life and Timeless Connections

A Halo Publishing International Anthology

BECAUSE
LOVE
REMAINS

Stories of Life and Timeless Connections

Halo PUBLISHING INTERNATIONAL

Halo
PUBLISHING
INTERNATIONAL

Halo Publishing International
7550 W IH-10 #800, PMB 2069,
San Antonio, TX 78229

First Edition, September 2025
ISBN: 978-1-63765-808-6
Library of Congress Control Number: 2025914549

Halo Publishing International is a self-publishing company that publishes adult fiction and non-fiction, children's literature, self-help, spiritual, and faith-based books. We continually strive to help authors reach their publishing goals and provide many different services that help them do so. We do not publish books that are deemed to be politically, religiously, or socially disrespectful, or books that are sexually provocative, including erotica. Halo reserves the right to refuse publication of any manuscript if it is deemed not to be in line with our principles. Do you have a book idea you would like us to consider publishing? Please visit www.halopublishing.com for more information.

Acknowledgements

We extend our heartfelt gratitude to every individual who has made a contribution to this book:

Roberto Alfaro
Renato Bettio
Donna Bond
Lisa Cassman
Irene Roth
Lisa Michelle Umina
Bethany Zare

Foreword

To be running breathlessly, but not yet arrived,
is itself delightful, a suspended moment of living hope.

—Anne Carson, Eros the Bittersweet

Love doesn't follow one script. That's why love stories remain constant through time; sitting down to tell one is always an endless exploration. The forms love takes are unpredictable. It slips through our hands when we try to hold it too tightly, yet it leaves us changed whenever it passes through our lives.

When I think of love, I remember the blur of family photographs: my mother's laughter frozen mid-smile, my father's hand caught in motion, my own arms reaching toward a butterfly already gone. Those imperfect images somehow capture what love really feels like: fleeting, full of movement, impossible to possess. Love is not the stillness of a perfect picture; it is the motion just before it.

In this anthology, the authors invite us into their own living portraits of love. Each story is a moment caught in motion: the chance encounter that sparks a lifelong journey, the patient devotion that carries a marriage through time, the rediscovery of love after loss, or the surprising ways love transforms us when we least expect it. Together, these voices remind us that love is not one story, but many. And that it knows no labels—only souls, only humanity: two people, two lives meeting. Something as grand as love cannot be contained in words so simple.

Love, after all, is not only romance. It is resilience, the choice to keep showing up, the courage to remain open even when life has tested us. It is the audacity of movement—the blur we chase with the wonder of children—just as much as it is the quiet comfort of a familiar embrace.

As you read, you may see your own story reflected here: a memory of your first dance, the faith that carried you through hardship, the laughter you share with someone who knows you best. Or perhaps the ache of letting go, and the hope of finding love in a new form.

The truth is, no prologue can fully explain why we love, who we love, or how love endures. I cannot tell you what love is, but these stories offer something far more precious: an invitation to feel. To pause with each page and remember the love that has shaped you, the love you seek, the love you find, lose, long for, and the love still to come.

Between these covers, love has been captured not as an answer, but as a living blur of color, motion, and memory. Like a butterfly landing on your shoulder, it cannot be held forever. But for a moment, you can see it clearly. And that, in itself, is enough.

So here's to the mystery of love, to the stories that keep it alive, and to the voices of Roberto Alfaro, Renato Bettio, Donna Bond, Lisa Cassman, Irene Roth, Lisa Michelle Umina, and Bethany Zare. Thank you for catching the butterfly for us.

Camila Del Águila
Chief Editor of Halo Publishing International

Contents

Our Authors

Roberto and Anna

The One Salsa Dance That Changed Our Lives Forever

Roberto Alfaro

"I can't recite the words that were said on that special day… Or describe all the magic that was in the air on our wedding day… But the one thing that I'll always remember and will treasure in my heart for the rest of my life…is in knowing that on that memorable day… I married my best friend forever…my beautiful wife."

These words echoed once again, in May 2019, as we stood together and renewed our vows, celebrating twenty-five beautiful years of marriage. It was more than a ceremony—it was a tribute to a journey built on love, laughter, and timeless memories that shaped us as a couple.

It all began on an early winter night in 1991, when fate led me to the legendary Copacabana nightclub in the heart of New York City. For a salsa dancing enthusiast like me, it was the perfect escape—a place pulsating with lots of rhythm and energy.

That day, the moment I stepped onto the scene, I saw her—she was tall, radiant, and mesmerizing. Her presence alone lit up the dance floor. She wore elegance with a touch of allure, exuding what I called "a unique blend of Puerto Rican and European beauty" that made her stand out in every way. She was absolutely stunning and beautiful…beyond words.

Without hesitation, I asked her to dance. She smiled—just enough to send my heart racing—and said, "Sure." The DJ dropped a killer salsa track, and suddenly we were gliding across the dance floor as if we'd done this a thousand times before. One song turned into two, and we never looked back.

At the time, we had no idea what that one spontaneous dance would spark a love story that would grow, blossom, and carry us through more than three decades of life together. But what followed our first dance was a whirlwind of connection and discovery.

We officially became a couple on March 30, 1991, and from there on, love took the lead. And in May 1994, I married my beautiful queen in a wedding that captured both our passion for each other and the salsa rhythm that first united us as one.

Looking back now, we both believe it was destiny—an act of divine timing. Because as it turns out, neither one of us was even supposed to be there that night. But, somehow, we found ourselves in the right place, at the perfect moment—brought together by something greater than chance.

Thirty-four years later (thirty-one as husband and wife), we're still dancing—through life, through challenges, through joy. Our amazing bond is built on the smallest acts of love: saying "I love you" without reason, cracking up over the silliest things, or just being present for each other day after day.

We also cherish experiencing life side by side—romantic dinners, movie nights, workouts, long walks in the park. Embracing those warm hugs and kisses that mean the world to us. Every shared moment keeps our connection vibrant and deep.

And when it comes to celebrating special occasions, we go all in—surprise gifts, handwritten love notes, heartfelt cards, and poems. Outshone only by a deep and enduring love note displayed above our headboard; it reads, Always Kiss Me Good Night. A loving pledge that we take pride in honoring every day.

Yet, above all, we've also come to realize that over the years, many of the most joyful and meaningful moments in our lives have blossomed from surprising each other during special occasions. For these are the moments that steal our breath, linger in our hearts, and celebrate the deep-rooted love we share—the kind of magic that only comes from romantic and unforgettable surprises. And while our marriage is filled with countless cherished memories, here's just a short list of some of our all-time favorites.

A Surprise Within A Surprise

One year, for her birthday, I planned a surprise dinner at a beloved restaurant in Milford, Connecticut. Before I even made the reservation, I visited the place myself to meet up with the manager and share my plan. She listened closely, then broke into a wide smile and told me how honored she was that I'd chosen her restaurant to help make this evening unforgettable.

My girlfriend (at the time), Anna, was a huge Kenny G fan, so I had an idea. What if, during dinner, she was serenaded with her favorite song, "Going Home," played live on the saxophone? It felt like the perfect idea. But making it happen, I knew, wasn't going to be that simple.

Over the days that followed, I searched everywhere for the right saxophonist, one with both the skill and style to pull off such a meaningful piece. It was almost a lost cause until I stumbled upon a listing in a local Variety newspaper, advertising musicians available for weddings and events. One ad stood out from all the others, so I gave the gentleman a call. He was a jazz saxophonist who admitted he'd never played Kenny G before, but he was really intrigued. All he asked for was a few days to learn and rehearse the piece. And I agreed.

When he called me back days later to say he was ready, I was thrilled, yet a little nervous at the same time. What if it didn't sound right, and he was nowhere close to playing like Kenny G? Then what? Still, with no other options and plenty of hope, I hired him and shared all the details about when and how the surprise should unfold.

Well, to my surprise, it worked out perfectly. That day, right in the middle of dinner, he entered the restaurant and began to play. His saxophone filled the room with smooth, mesmerizing notes. For a moment, it felt as if Kenny G himself were there. I was really blown away—not just by the performance, but by the fact that this was his very first time playing that piece in public.

At first, my girlfriend assumed it was just the restaurant's live entertainment. She leaned over and said, "Wow, it's so cool that they have live jazz music tonight." But then recognition hit—she realized it was her favorite song. As the saxophonist made his way toward our table, her eyes widened, and she glanced at me with a look that said it all: Is this…for me?

It was. I grinned and said, "Happy birthday, babe—this is all for you!"

She blushed and covered her mouth in disbelief. As the musician got closer, the excitement spread beyond our table—other diners soon began to cheer and clap. Her reaction was priceless, and in that moment, I knew I'd pulled off something truly special. To top it off, the saxophonist seamlessly transitioned into "Happy Birthday," and the entire staff soon joined in to sing.

Then came the grand finale: a gorgeous birthday cake I'd secretly arranged to be delivered earlier. She closed her eyes, made a wish, and blew out the candles. The joy on her face that night said everything.

It was a celebration neither of us will ever forget—a moment that reminded me why I love surprising her in the first place. Well, that is...until the next big surprise comes around.

A Love Painted in Time: Our Second-Anniversary Surprise

To celebrate our one-year anniversary of being engaged, I wanted to gift my future wife something unforgettable—something that captured both our past and our beautiful future together. I found the perfect way: having a custom airbrush painting created by a seasoned artist who'd spent years crafting portraits by hand.

My vision? A nearly life-size painting based on a photo of us from the early days of dating, paired with a smaller portrait just above it—this time, featuring us in wedding outfits, standing proudly beside a white Excalibur limo.

When I shared this idea with the artist, he smiled and said, "No problem! Just give me a couple of weeks." I left giddy with anticipation, imagining how moved my fiancée would be when she saw it. I wanted her to see herself dressed as a bride—to dream it, feel it, and know it was all becoming real.

Two weeks later…

The finished piece took my breath away. Not only had the artist nailed our likenesses, but he'd transformed a modest four-by-six photo from 1991 into a vivid portrait of our future wedding day. And I knew just where to unveil it—the very restaurant where we'd first celebrated our engagement, a place called Jalapeno Heaven, in Branford, Connecticut.

That day, I met up with the manager, who was really overjoyed we'd chosen her space again to celebrate our one-year engagement anniversary. She promised us the same table and happily agreed to hang the painting on the wall behind us.

Setting the scene…

On the morning of our anniversary, I returned to the restaurant to prepare the surprise. I hung the portrait with care and then added a bold purple ribbon diagonally from corner to corner. I also dressed the table with matching purple cloth and placed a bouquet of white and purple flowers in the center—echoing the colors our bridesmaids would wear.

Then I slipped away to await our dinner reservation.

The reveal…

That evening, as we walked in and followed the waitress to our table, my beautiful fiancée spotted the display. Her face quickly lit up with joy and disbelief. She stood stunned, smiling widely as the warmth and love in the room quickly wrapped around her. All she could say was "Wow, babe…how the heck did you do this? This is amazing!!! I absolutely love it!!!"

That night, we toasted with wine, savoring dinner and soaking in all the love from the staff and nearby patrons who stopped by to congratulate us. Most importantly, we talked about our wedding and how that one single portrait captured the dream we were building. It was more than a gift—it was a vision, a memory in progress, and a celebration of everything we'd become.

So with full hearts and raised glasses, we made our toast: "Here's to us on our anniversary…two hearts, one love, and one very special moment. I love you with all my heart and soul, babe!"

And last, but certainly not least, pulling off one of the biggest surprises ever...

The Jennifer Lopez Surprise

In February 2018, we were in Las Vegas to celebrate my beautiful wife's fiftieth birthday. That evening, we had tickets to see JLo perform at the Zappos Theater in the Planet Hollywood Resort and Casino.

As part of the celebration, unbeknownst to her, I wrote a little note that read, "Happy 50th Birthday, Anna!" I tucked it into my wallet before heading to the show, hoping I might find someone behind the scenes who could pass it along to JLo—just maybe she'd give my wife a special birthday shout-out onstage.

When we arrived, I spotted a couple of Las Vegas police officers working the event. While my wife waited in line, I approached them, flashed my badge, and introduced myself as a retired officer. I explained what I was hoping to do and asked if they had any connections to JLo's team who could make this wonderful surprise happen. They were super kind and apologetic—but, unfortunately, they didn't know anyone who could help pull off this surprise. I gracefully thanked them both and turned my thoughts to hopefully finding someone else inside the theater instead.

We were seated right in the middle of the second-level tier, about twenty rows back from the stage. I quickly noticed three crew members behind us who appeared to be in charge of handling the lighting and sound for the show. I told my wife I'd be right back, then approached one of them. Once again, I made my pitch. And, once again, I struck out—apparently they weren't "allowed to pass along any personal requests."

Disappointed, but still hopeful, I returned back to my seat and finally decided to tell my wife about the surprise I had tried to pull off. When I showed her the little handwritten note, her eyes lit up with joy and disbelief. "Aww, babe, that's the sweetest thing! You didn't have to do that...but thank you so, so much. I love you!"

Moments later, I happened to glance to my right and instantly recognized a familiar face walking our way. I turned to my wife and said, "Babe, I think that's Benny Medina—JLo's manager!" She was skeptical at first, but when he sat down just one seat away from us, we couldn't resist Googling him. And, sure enough, it was Benny.

I realized it was now or never, so I decided to approach him. I quickly introduced myself and asked if he might be able to ask JLo to wish my wife a happy birthday from the stage. I even added a bit of background to show I wasn't just a fan—I'd appeared briefly in Maid in Manhattan as a party guest dancing with one of the principal actresses in the movie. I also added that my wife once lived on the same Bronx-neighborhood street as JLo did back in the day.

Benny smiled and said, "Wow, that's pretty cool, Roberto." But, unfortunately, he said he couldn't make the birthday shout-out happen…but he had something even better in mind. He offered us a backstage meet-and-greet with JLo after the concert.

I was floored. I shook his hand and thanked him sincerely. When I shared the news with my wife, she was stunned. "Babe, there's no way… Are you serious?"

I grinned and said, "Absolutely, babe. Happy fiftieth birthday!" We hugged and kissed, soaking in all the magic and blessings from that special moment.

After the show, just as promised, Benny's team led us backstage, where we had the once-in-a-lifetime chance to meet JLo in person. Not only did we snap a few photos, but she also wished my wife a heartfelt "Happy fiftieth birthday" face-to-face. I thanked both JLo and Benny for their incredible kindness—an unforgettable gift. A night that neither of us will ever, ever forget.

That moment was the cherry on top of an already-extraordinary week for my beautiful queen. It had begun with a surprise birthday party at our daughter Bianca's house in California, followed by an appearance on America's Funniest Home Videos, where we got to hang out backstage with the host, Alfonso Ribeiro (whom I'd been assigned to escort as a Hartford Connecticut Police Officer, back in the early '90s when he visited Hartford), and were even featured on national TV. From there, we took a trip to Vegas, caught a Matt Franco magic show—where my wife was even invited onstage for a few tricks—and finally met JLo.

What can I say? It was truly an incredible, unreal fiftieth-birthday celebration of surprises that turned out better than we could've ever imagined. All thanks to God and all those beautiful blessings that have filled our lives with unforgettable moments, cherished memories, and love that continues to amaze us to this day.

But, more anything, we are extremely grateful and thankful for that "one salsa dance." That one day ignited the magical spark between us and led us on this wonderful journey and adventure...that I get to enjoy with the love of my life.

Renato and Doreen

An Interesting Journey

Renato Bettio

—'Nas tardes, 'ña Licha.

—'Nas tardes, Corinita. How you've been? What's poppin'?

—I'm hanging, as they say. Earlier today, I was reading something Paul told the Corinthians ages ago, to make them behave. Yes, let me tell you, those Corinthians knew, even then, what love is. Do you, 'ña Licha, know what love is?

—The things you say, Corinita! Seems like you enjoy embarrassing people. Those things, they are private. Sounds like those so-called Corinthians might've been weirdos.

—How come, 'ña Licha! Love is for everyone, *pues*. And so Paul says.

—If you say so, well, it must be true. But I do suggest you don't go around saying that love is for everyone. You might be misunderstood, pues. Small minds have only small ideas, you know.

—Look at you! I didn't know you were a philosopher, 'ña Licha.

—Well, now you know. If you ever need advice, here I am.

* * * * *

Definitions, definitions... To define, we delve our senses into the wells of thought. There are millions of them. Each one filled with the definition of a particular sensation, idea, desire. Defining is comparing. Comparing needs understanding. Understanding needs presence—one must be present in will, present in duty.

Let's say, for example, that we are asked to define love. We dive, then, into one of those wells, the one labeled "LOVE." We fill our crate with definitions; we count them, even the ones that fell out of the crate in our haste to fill it with a few thousand more definitions that are next in the queue. (That next person is just as impatient. They just saw that you dropped a bunch of definitions, and they want those for their crate, for themselves.)

So we walk away with our crate filled with definitions of love. We sit, and one by one take out the definitions. First the ones that we like better, those that hit just the spot, the smart ones; then the ones we frown upon, the ugly ones, to discard. Because we like to be called smart, to seem smart. At the bottom of the crate, only a couple of definitions are left. One of them is your wife's; the other one is yours (of course, yours is the best of them all). But then, left untouched, there at the bottom, is Paul's.

This one was written by an abuser, a violent persecutor who, with clean blows, subjugated all believers of the newest religion that eventually would change the world. So you read it and think, *This one's pretty good*. You take it as an example, a platform from which to change, from which to improve your very own definition (yes, the *best* of them all).

You are left with three definitions: Paul's, your wife's, and yours.

The value of your wife's definition of love is that it is unwritten but perceived, felt. Its value grows with the passing of the years. Your definition changes with the closeness of your wife's definition, and you begin to observe that said definition encompasses, weaves, and attracts other feelings, experiences. And without even noticing, you are led to a final definition that takes all others into account.

A day like any other, you look back upon the first moment your path began, when you found your partner, the one who, through stormy times, would make living a bit smoother. She helped you create a new definition of love, and with that, you forged the best of the paths available for you through the fruits of your labor, achieving a place in your community and at the table upon which your alms are served. She helped you make amends for your mistakes, even when you believed you had nothing for which to atone, and she even forgave you all transgressions. She took care of you when you were sick, and will do so again once your steps become difficult in old age. She gifted you the marvel of being called Father and will hold your hands when you are forced to bid farewell to those who are called to leave. She has never asked for anything for herself, and, thanks to her, you have the opportunity and the right to firmly step into the midst of the many beings, whose brains cultivate multitudes of definitions for love, and say with a confident, warm voice, "I know how to add to the definitions of love, even to the one Paul wrote two thousand years ago, because I learned it from my wife through the years." And then you affirm, "Love is staying, remaining…in spite of it all."

Yet, the critic replies, "Very well then, you gave us a definition of love that refers to what your wife stands for, what she means to you, and what she has expressed throughout the years. Now tell us about your own perception of love between people."

Dear critic, what breeds in solitude needs no help. Companionship can be found anywhere. So let's say, then, that judging is easier in solitude. So, which is the best starting point from which to receive a response to your questions?

A suggestion: This must be our duty, our challenge; suffering must, daily, be the stone in our shoe, for we need no answers in happiness. And happiness is so scarce! Happy moments are fleeting, and yet they remind us there will be an end to our suffering. So, by overcoming, you are rewarded with success. You'll need no more.

Let's remember: When we are young and beside us walks the one who will forever unite our lives as one, that partner is, generally, poor, or mostly poor, in terms of their capacity to obtain what they need to live. They know exactly where that little twenty-five-cent coin is because that coin will be needed to buy at the store what-ever their children need.

These challenges of life bid you to unite and take care of each other in order to move forward and conquer. Years go by, and by working hard, you get out of that pseudo poverty. The moment arrives when you no longer need to know where that coin is, because the challenge has been overcome through united uniting efforts. Thus, you are both happy about your achievements and what they mean to you and, more importantly, to your children.

Therefore, this would be my definition of love: to persist in positive character and honest work, without complaint, until your smile reflects the knowledge that those who you take care of have no needs.

* * * * *

I'll talk about another kind of love, one that is indescribable and powerful, one that has remained inviolate throughout the generations. Noble love. Love for your profession, which can be your destiny too. Love that, when finally put on a scale, will outweigh anything placed opposite it.

So, let's guess and say there is an instructor who pours his life into teaching the poor to read, and as the teacher reaches the end of his life, those who were taught by him number in the thousands, an untold number of good men and women. These people, let's say, become scientists, academics, religious leaders, just because they were taught to read by this man in the dark classrooms of a poor school.

Now, let's imagine that said teacher, who never had a perfect family life or social life, on a day like any other, dies or is killed, and his duties as an instructor forever stop. No more teaching, no more reaching for the virtue of knowledge.

What, then, will be the reward for such a person? Does his private life's mistakes outweigh the undeniable trials he overcame and the good he did for generations to come? For it is undeniable that, because of him, his students learned there is a God, they wrote poetry and produced works of art that will live on long after their deaths, and humanity has inherited a rich legacy…again, just because of him.

You who know how to read these lines because someone taught you the magic of the written word, tell me, what is more significant? And let me answer that anything that can change the path of a life, directing it to that which is good—love—is powerful and supreme.

Yet there is nothing like the love you receive from the being who gave you life. Even Paul falls short. If we truly think about it, if we transcend Paul's words, we will deduce that it is not a single being but a pair of people who gave us life. With that life came the freedom to return, through our actions, the favor to thank them for the life we freely got.

The love that washes over us from these beings slips by without a sound. Its goal is not to attract attention to itself. As someone once said about that kind of love, "The silence of a mother's love for their offspring speaks louder than a thousand trumpets."

Let's not be shy in our judgments. Memory and intelligence are treasures gifted by nature. Any diminishment in them, even seemingly insignificant, will affect the ability to fulfill our duties. Science has developed so much in the past years, to the point of grasping the causes of this diminishment and the appropriate treatments for it. Cancer and other physiological dysfunctions are difficult to overcome, even though science offers cures and treatments that will extend our lifespan. But these are the challenges we will face as our bodies age. They can't, or shouldn't, be faced alone. Love and affection walk in with prodigious goodwill. Those who love and are loved live and conquer, be it poverty, sickness, or life's never-ending challenges and fears.

Love—that undeniable force gifted to our spirit by the Supreme Kindness—is invincible because it is immeasurable. Its presence fills the unwritten spaces across our soul when we, or those we love, get ready to overcome a challenge. And so, victory, success, is more attainable, more probable, and the path is smoother when you walk with someone who, with kind words and actions, makes the fight less wearisome and gives you the will to continue without blaming the Creator for your misfortunes. A companion, with just a few words, can lift our inner child out of a corner of pity and help us dissolve senseless resolutions.

Lord, Lord, we've been told countless times to give it a last shot, to drain ourselves to the last drop of passion, because the gates to glory open only when we insist, when we continue stubbornly knocking on the doors.

Paul and Donna

The One

Donna Bond

Once in a while,
in the middle of an ordinary life,
love gives us a fairy tale.

—Lila DiPasqua

I was miserable after ending a relationship that looked good on paper but wasn't The One. I felt ostracized by my friends and family for breaking it off. He was a handsome, accomplished, wonderful man, and we had dated for a year and a half. He was caring, charming, successful, and according to my mother, as she watched me approach forty, "He would have taken care of you for the rest of your life."

No matter how much it seemed too good to be true, there was something in our energetics that never meshed into a perfect match. He was a military guy. I was a spiritual dreamer. I used to tell him all the time, *"You need to learn how to color outside the lines!"* I said this to him repeatedly. I even left a love note and a twenty-four pack of Crayola magic markers on the dashboard of his car as my not-so-subtle hint to help him get the point.

I stayed in the relationship for a year and a half because it was easy and entertaining. But not because I loved this man enough to be his forevermore. In five months, I will be turning forty years old. I knew I was wasting time, and despite zero other options, I did the uncomfortable thing and broke it off. I knew in my soul he wasn't The One.

Feeling lonely, miserable, and physically sick from being banished by my own loved ones for ending this promising prospect, I remembered the brochure I picked up earlier in my spiritual bookstore. I pulled it out and read about a modality called Body Talk and a woman named Lee Ann.

At the ridiculously late hour of 11:30 p.m.—on Valentine's Day, no less—I called Lee Ann. She answered. I said I needed to see her, and we made an appointment for Saturday. We hung up quickly.

I took a deep breath. For some reason, I felt better. I distinctly remember thinking to myself, *I can relax because I know she is going to help me.* I just lay there and cried.

On Friday, February 15, I logged into my Match.com account. Exercising the usual protocol, I deleted most of the emails and winks I had received over the past week. But there was one who got my attention.

Feb 13

> *I am a Laguna Beach native and after many years away from the coast living here in Santa Fe, NM, have decided to move back to California. Hopefully to Laguna Beach. In the process I was curious to see who was swimming around in the Match pool and saw you splashing around. You're adorable. And the fact that you like Carolyn Myss is very cool. Her work has changed the way I look at the world. Anyway, good luck to you in this journey…*
>
> *Paul*

I was instantly intrigued that someone would write to me about Caroline Myss, my favorite American author of books about mysticism and wellness. And while my profile revealed she was my favorite author, I had not mentioned that I was currently reading her book *Sacred Contracts*. Something in me stirred, and I felt a glimmer of hope as I remembered that tomorrow would be the day I would see medical intuitive Lee Ann.

I took the next step and clicked through to his profile. I read Mr. Santa Fe's Match.com rundown. I felt a bit of wonder and intrigue. There seemed to be a lot of energy resonating inside of me. I combed through his details, sniffing out any red flags or danger signs. I was pissed that he lived in New Mexico and thought, *I can't get involved in another long-distance relationship!* In my mind, I heard the stern voice of reason. *I'm not going to respond to this guy.*

The headline of his profile announced, "Looking for The One." Admittedly, it gave me pause, but the long-distance thing really would be a problem. I got to the last line of his profile. It was an open-jawed mic drop. Not responding was no longer an option. ***"I am looking for a woman who is willing to color outside the lines; you know who you are."***

It felt as if someone were playing a joke on me. My stomach did a flip-flop. I literally looked around my living room as if I were being watched. It felt a little bit shocking and beyond serendipitous that Mr. Santa Fe's profile had this sentiment as his last line.

Reluctantly, I did respond. My note was short and a little bit flippant.

Feb 15

So, when are you coming back to SoCal?

I was just online booking a conference in New York in which Caroline Myss is the keynote.

I'm looking for someone with like-minded values and who can make me laugh as hard as you advertise in

*your profile. Plus, my motto is that I do color outside
the lines.*

Donna

Saturday, February 16, I went to see Lee Ann. I walked into her little room at the Soul Spa, a new age bookstore, and said hello. We didn't speak much. I got on her table, and for the next two hours, Lee Ann murmured to herself with that delicious South African accent, using my right arm as a sort of electrical conductor. She smelled like chocolate and vanilla, and I felt very safe in her care.

She tried to explain to me the information she was getting; she presumably was having a conversation with Spirit simultaneously. She mentioned my depression. I wasn't even really sure that's what it was until she said it, but then I was. She said there was some big event that had happened in my life between the ages of twenty and twenty-three, and something happening now triggered that event.

It made so much sense! The event at age twenty-two was the death of my father. The trigger was the breakup with my boyfriend, and the emotional and physical pain was overwhelming feelings of grief and loss.

Lee Ann was balancing and linking stuff. I have no idea what she did, nor did I need to know. There was a strange element of trust present, and I just went with it. After the session, with tears streaming down my face,

I told Lee Ann, "*I just need to find The One. I just broke up with a great guy, and he was wonderful, but he was not The One. I need to find The One.*"

I left in a very peaceful space. I felt balanced, happy, and calm. It was surreal. She gave me a magic bottle of water called Aqua Mantra that had infused messages of "I am loved" all in it. I felt it. I felt it from Lee Ann, and from the whole universe.

That night, I checked my email again, and there was another message from Paul waiting for me.

Feb 15

Hi Donna,

I will be back there within the next few weeks to visit family in San Diego, see my friend in Laguna, and explore moving back.

So what's the conference in NY w/Caroline Myss? I am in New York somewhat regularly, visiting my son. If I were there at the time, I would love to see her.

The last book I read of hers was Sacred Contracts. It inspired a series of paintings I did called Sacred Contracts. They are on my website if you're interested: www.paulbondart.com. I thought of sending her a painting, or at least e-mailing her the images. But I don't know how accessible she is, so I never tried. I don't want to appear a Caroline Myss groupie!

Maybe when I get to CA in the next weeks we can meet for a coffee or soda pop somewhere overlooking the ocean…if you're so inclined.

Ciao, Paul

P.S. I had the feeling you were a "color outside the lines" kind of girl, which is why I was moved to write you.

I responded.

I was FREAKING OUT that the last book he read was *Sacred Contracts* because I had it next to my bedstand!

Feb 16

Hi Paul,

I'm leaving for a conference tomorrow, so emails may be sparse this week. You're a grandpa? I'm turning forty at the end of March! I went to a medical intuitive today using Body Talk - she was mind-blowing. I had awful sleep issues for months, and in one session, she helped me. I feel totally different - there's actually light shining from my eyes.

Isn't the universe grand?

I'm glad we connected.

Donna

I awoke the next morning after a deep and peaceful sleep. It was a miracle. I looked in the mirror, and I said out loud to myself, "Well, hello there, I remember you." I felt amazing! I couldn't get over it. I felt like my old self was reborn. The work with LeeAnn transformed me inside and out. I am convinced this profound and necessary rejuvenation was a cosmic intervention opening a sacred portal for the unfolding of this fairy tale.

I'm not sure I'll ever be able to explain what Lee Ann does, but it's unimportant. I just know I was transformed. The following day, in a room full of women, they all reflected on my incredible shift. *"Donna, you look great. You're glowing. What happened to you? You seem radiant compared to when we saw you last week?"* They were witnesses to my previous deterioration and now my soulful rejuvenation.

Paul and I exchanged emails for almost a month before we met in person on March 9, 2008. Hundreds of documented emails were lovingly exchanged between us, leading to the divine appointment our souls were arranging. It felt as if it was the unfolding of our souls' history that only we could sense and understand. It was the rebirth of a sacred contract.

Before we met, I was invited into another deep recharge. My soul sister Stacy called and simply said, "Get here." I booked a flight to Palm Beach Gardens without question, knowing somehow it was all preparation leading me to him. The One.

Palm Beach was more deep-soul preparation. No deadlines, no pressure, no one at work needing my attention. The biggest decision I had to face for seven days was what to eat for dinner. I got to giggle with my friend and fantasize about my destined encounter with Mr. Santa Fe. I let my imagination run wild every night for a week, dreaming him into reality.

The flirting was coy. The anticipation built. The sexual tension was real. The feeling in my heart and soul was one of fulfillment and gratitude. He mailed me a playlist that he created and burned onto a CD for me. This musical love letter set the backdrop, staged the scene, and tended the nuanced details. All I had to do was fall.

Fall into him.

The whole unfolding, I just knew. When I bought new 400-thread-count Egyptian cotton sheets, I knew. When I was dancing in my pajamas in front of the mirror, giggling each night while Sting's "She Walks" blasted through my iPod headset, I knew. When I'd feel aroused in the middle of the day just from hearing the sound of his voice over the phone, I knew. When his emails seemed to be reading my mind, and my face hurt from smiling so much, I knew.

The journal I kept during that soul-preparation vacation captured all I knew before we even met. I documented with great clarity that he was, in fact, *The One*.

That morning, he phoned.

My heart sank a little with a brief but large wave of panic, as fear tried to tempt me into thinking, *What if he's calling to say he isn't coming?*

He called to confirm our plans.

The Sunday of that sacred union, my entire day existed for the moment we would meet. I set the scene on the San Clemente beach, not far from my home, with a purple duvet and little yellow flowers. Crisp white wine and a little fruit and cheese. For giggles, I included a whole eggplant with my beach setup. This symbol was a humorous nod to my Italian heritage, inspired by Michael Franks's playful song about being smitten with an Italian woman and her culinary talents. It was one of many musical backdrops from the love letter playlist I binged repeatedly so I could feel that emotional intimacy close the physical distance between us.

I sat patiently on that purple duvet. I knew I was early, and I knew he'd be late, but it didn't matter; I would have waited there forever.

My mind was lovingly entwined in the romance of the day, going over all the details. Running errands and finding gems along the way to celebrate this soul reunion, making it as memorable as possible. To the mall to get a stereo connector for the iPod. Breeze by the shoe store and find a corked pair of black patent-leather wedges. Round the corner past the local boutique shop, and in the window I see the sweetest white silk blouse with a perfect white satin bow. I grab it in a rush. I don't try it on because I know it's perfect.

It all falls into place. The salesgirl adds a white jacket for safe measure, knowing we will be on the beach. She marvels at me as I tell her I'm about to meet my soulmate.

I gazed in awe over all the pieces falling perfectly into place as I waited on that purple duvet to meet *The One*. Recounting all our emails from the last thirty days. Remembering all the emotions. Peeking back over several pages in my journal sitting next to me like a loyal witness to this divine unfolding. Rereading the free-flowing vision from my journal that I had written a long while ago about the man I *was dreaming up*. I sat in fascination, realizing he fit every single thing I had written!

I waited.

I kept my back to the sun and towards the direction I knew he'd approach me. I wanted to let him surprise me. I can't remember my thoughts when he said hello, but I will never forget my heart skipping a beat at seeing his shadow cast over me, projected onto the duvet. The scene is etched in my heart forever. My soul knew *he had returned. He had come home. He was here.*

I took a deep breath, slowly turning around. He fell to his knees. I went up on mine. Simultaneously, we took off our sunglasses like a Hollywood movie scene. With reverence, we met the other's gaze with passion and intensity as we faced knee to knee on the sand-covered duvet.

I told him, *"You're late."* We laughed and embraced with tears in our eyes. I felt so much emotion pouring from my heart and welling through my chest. Looking into his eyes for the first time, and seeing into his soul again, the clarity was profound. He found me. *I know you,* rang from our hearts with remembrance.

Our first night together was beautiful. Watching the sun go down, having dinner in a little Italian restaurant, sleeping next to each other without yet making love. I will remember every bit of nervousness, every heart-beat, every moment always. I can't say that I fell in love with him then because I was already in love. Before we met, before all the emails, before this lifetime, he was always my love.

We held each other as if we were making up for lost time. We both knew we were. No one else would believe it, but we had been reunited. We exchanged passionate kisses and felt each other's bodies through our clothes. The next morning, we woke up asking each other, *"Is this real?"* It felt like Christmas.

Off to work, I had to report. By 11:00 a.m., the roses arrived. I stood at the front desk, trembling. I couldn't believe it. I hugged the big vase of red roses with the big red bow, cradling them as if I were holding a baby. It certainly felt as though a birth was occurring. The card said, "You left me speechless...Paolo."

I came home from work and found a note on my kitchen counter. It read, "I simply love you." It was with a Ylang Ylang scratch and sniff, and the remote control to the CD player. I hit play. Cue Michael Franks's "I Hope It's You."

Thirty days later, on my fortieth birthday, on that same beach in San Clemente, Paul proposed to me without a ring or a plan or a clue. I said YES, never having been so sure of anything in my life. When you know, you know.

My mother was freaking out. My boss was running background checks. Everybody thought I'd lost my mind. "Donna! What are you doing? You met this guy on the internet!!!?" We stayed engaged for a year so everyone else would chill out. But we knew.

Paul and I have been married now for seventeen years. Our sacred contract was necessary for each one of us to fulfill our purpose in this life. If not for me, he wouldn't have gone on to become a professional fine artist. If it weren't for him, I wouldn't have found my way to becoming a soul catalyst and spiritual psychology coach.

Sometimes I think about that distraught woman who was lying on the couch on Valentine's Day in 2008, and I want to whisper to her, "Trust the process. The divine design is unfolding. The universe is conspiring to bring you exactly what you need."

Once in a while, in the middle of an ordinary life, love gives us a fairy tale. Ours is still being written.

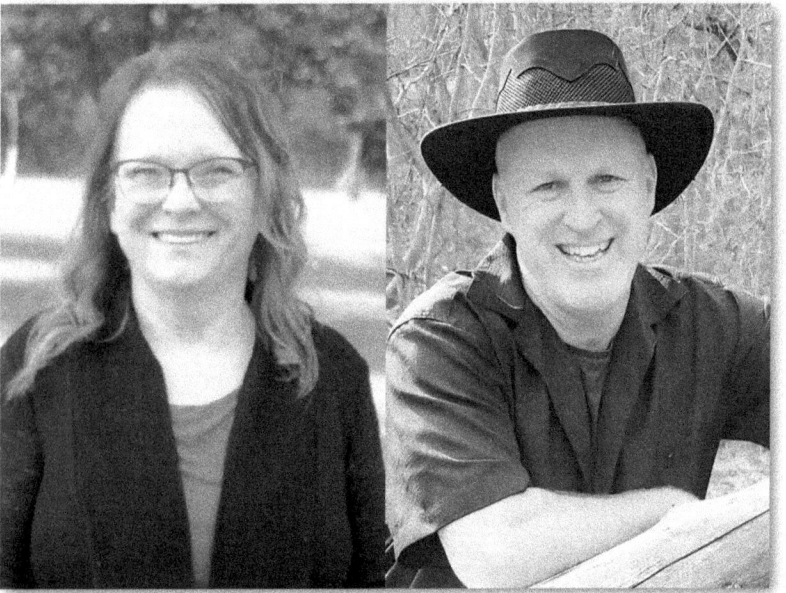

Lisa and Steve

Our Love Story, Our Day from Camp

Lisa Cassman

I t took all of me to hit the Send button. It had been twenty-five years since I had had any contact with him… Looking at the photo that was taken of us, I was hoping that I had finally found him.

Thinking back over all those years, to when I was a teen, I remember him asking me to the banquet at Teen Bible Camp. I was shy, and he was really good-looking (he still is). I wondered why, of all the girls there, he asked me. I didn't know him, as he was from a different town, and I wondered if I would ever see him again, even if I did attend the banquet with him. Nevertheless, I decided to go with him.

That evening was fun. I don't remember exactly what we talked about, but I do know I felt like someone special for the first time in my life. I wondered often if I had made him feel the same way.

The next summer, I saw him again at the same camp. After that, we kept in contact for a few years, but he eventually went into the army, and we lost contact with one another.

I started writing poetry about how I felt about him and later published the collection in my book *The Light in Your Eyes*. I didn't want to forget him, but I did eventually get married and give birth to two sons. I kept busy taking care of life's details, being a wife and mother, and working full time.

My first marriage eventually ended, and life had to just move along. Finally, I felt relaxed and took it day by day. I eventually learned how to search online for people, and I did just that.

I found and called his parents, but they wouldn't give me any information about him. I wondered if I would ever be able to find him. I wanted to just chat and see how he was doing and what he was up to. Then after a short time, I finally came to the conclusion that maybe I could look on social media for the one I had a crush on so many years ago.

I saw his name, and I was pretty sure I had found him. I would have to wait and see. After some time, I wrote a brief message asking if he was the one who was at Bible camp and asked me to the banquet. I wanted to make sure I had the correct guy. Nervously, I finally clicked the Send button, hoping I had the right man and he would reply.

I waited all weekend, but he finally answered and said that, yes, he was the guy. I felt as if I were a teenager all over again. He wasn't married at the time, so that was perfect for me. We reconnected and started talking about our lives and what we had done since we lost contact. I found out he had also been married and had two sons.

After a time of only communicating, we started planning some events together. We had a lot of fun that summer, going to events such as the Minnesota State Fair, the Renaissance Festival, county fairs, and meeting the families. We even went back to the camp and recreated the photo taken so long ago. What fun, fond memories. I enjoyed going back to where we first met.

We eventually planned a trip to Duluth, Minnesota, and the Two Harbors area in October. It was so much fun, and the weather was beautiful. We took walks and enjoyed the great outdoors. We climbed the Enger Tower, went on the zip line, and ate at some great restaurants.

That weekend, Steve proposed to me on the rocks by the lake at Lutsen Resort. It was on October 10, 2010 (10/10/10), at 10:10 a.m. It was a nice, romantic getaway. We then drove to Gooseberry Falls, which was absolutely breathtaking.

As we were taking a walk, we saw a lighthouse and asked a gentleman to take our photo, as we had just got engaged. He turned out to be a professional photographer. What an amazing weekend we had.

We planned our wedding in just two short months and got married outdoors on December 18, a cold winter day. It was in Brainerd, Minnesota, at an arboretum decorated with outdoor Christmas lights. We were able to have our wedding under the lights shaped like a tunnel. It was small and intimate, with only close friends and family in attendance. Afterwards, we all drove through the rest of the beautiful light display. It may have been cold outside, but my heart sure was warm. That day was the beginning of the rest of our lives together.

Steve had been driving a truck for twenty-five-plus years, so he was gone a lot when we first were married. It wasn't the easiest for me to be home alone in an unknown neighborhood. So I looked forward to him coming home each week; at this time, he was only gone a week at a time. Later, he would be gone two to three weeks at a time.

Soon after we were married, I rode in the truck with Steve for a short run. I enjoyed spending time with him. It was a local run, so we didn't go too far. After a while, he was offered a job out west, in Fontana, California. It wasn't the easiest decision, but he decided to accept the offer. We put most of our things in storage and drove to California with the car loaded, to have it out there, as we were going to live in the truck for six months.

While we were in California, I was with him in the truck twenty-four hours a day. At times, we stayed in the local motel or traveled in the car to beautiful places. I was able to see places I had never seen before, such as the scenery in Arizona, Nevada, and California, to mention a few. Riding in the truck with him changed my outlook on life, as the time with him was adventurous.

I like how he treated me and cared about my feelings. This is what a relationship should be like. While in the truck, I started writing a list of the things that he would do for me and how he treated me. Eventually, those scribblings became *The Road Less Traveled: A Guide to a Positive Marriage*, my first published book.

As we spent time together, we realized that we are complete opposites in choices of food, music, movies, and TV shows, to name a few. Not to mention that he would be warm while I was cold from the air-conditioning. There are a few things that we could definitely agree upon, though. One is going to church and knowing the importance of having God as a priority in our lives and our marriage. Another thing we agree on is taking walks; we both love the outdoors and enjoy seeing God's creation and wildlife.

Our lives may be different, but we are both willing to compromise. We build each other up and encourage one another. I wouldn't have been able to publish ten books or earn my PhD without his continued support. He was also very supportive of me when I wanted to open a salon/spa, and he still encourages me in my business. We feel we are perfect for each other, even though we know neither one of us is perfect. We have our disagreements, but we work through them. As they say, pick your battles.

We understand the need for feelings and being able to share them. Whether it is sadness, happy thoughts, joy, or just wanting to share the events of the day. One of the biggest things that attracted me to him was that he communicates with me. I feel, in a relationship, you need to trust, to communicate, and to keep going on dates. Don't let that get away from you. One of my favorite things to do is to have conversations while traveling. Yes, sometimes I may ramble on, but he still listens to what I have to say.

I enjoy going to events and speaking to women's groups where I can sell my books. He is right there with me to help set up the tent and table. Knowing you have a partner who is willing to move mountains and help you get somewhere in life is a great feeling of love and encouragement. We don't have high expectations, yet we each know what the other is capable of doing. It's not take-take-take, but give-and-take. Love has boundaries, trust, and respect. It is not an excuse to take each other for granted, but an opportunity to encourage, be kind, and, most of all, love.

Marriage can be difficult, some days more than others. But you can make it work as long as you both put in the effort. There are times when you may not feel your partner wants to do or is doing anything for you, but then think of the times they wanted to help, but you wouldn't accept it because you wanted to feel independent. Can you accept that it's okay to need and allow others to help you? Stay humble.

Here are just a few ways we respect and value one another:

1. We say, "I love you," and mean it. When you say something out of habit or pity, it doesn't sound real or genuine.

2. We say, "Thank you," when something is done for us. Appreciation goes a long way.

3. We go on dates, not just as husband and wife, but still as boyfriend and girlfriend. Always remember the moments when you first started dating.

4. We apologize when we are wrong or have been hurtful. It's not always easy to admit, but it will strengthen you and your marriage.

5. We support one another emotionally and spiritually, encouraging one another to attend church even on the hardest days to go.

These are just some of the ideas in *The Road Less Traveled: A Guide to a Positive Marriage.*

We both love one another's children. All of my biological grandchildren call and think of him as Grandpa, and he has definitely come to consider all of them his grandchildren. They are "our" grandkids.

No matter what happens in our life, I feel we will always have a great understanding and love for one another. I won't look back with regret. I will only look forward with the love that we will forever keep working on. Each day, I can say I love him more than the day before, as he keeps surprising me by showing me something that I didn't expect from him.

We have a great deal of respect for each other's family. The times spent with our families have been and are very important to both of us. In the years we have been married, we have each lost a parent, and the support we have shown each other through it all has been vital to lending the strength we needed at the time.

Steve is now home every day; he still drives a truck, but it is nice to see him and spend any moment with him that I can. He keeps me on my toes by making me laugh, even if I sometimes roll my eyes at him; he has an amazing sense of humor. It's the small things that matter to us both. Neither one of us is high maintenance, and we value our time together. Money can't buy time. We lost many years when we were apart, but that time taught us what we wanted in a relationship. No regrets—just moving forward with the love we now share.

Jim and Irene

A Divine Encounter

Irene Roth

W ho would have thought that a chance encounter would be long-lasting and marriage would result? Life has its own way of surprising us, especially when we feel as if nothing will ever change in our lives. There are moments of inexplicable divine intervention when God puts His mighty hand into our lives and blesses us.

These are usually moments that are completely out of our hands, no matter how much we plan or dream or hope. And sometimes, all we can do is trust that something bigger is at work. Call it fate, the universe, or what I've come to know as divine intervention. That's the only way I can explain how Jim and I met. I couldn't have orchestrated it even if I had tried.

It was the start of a brand-new year in January 2002. The streets of Stratford were blanketed with a fresh sprinkling of snow sparkling under the pale morning sun. Life outside looked still and beautiful, but inside my apartment on Greenwood, the stillness felt heavy. My Christmas decorations still lingered in the corners—fading red bows, a wilting poinsettia, the pine-scented candle that had lost its strong aroma. The holidays were over, and with them went the fleeting illusion of joy. It was back to reality, and mine was a quiet and solitary one.

I was forty, single, and had no reason to believe I wouldn't always be. My friends had long since married, had children, and were now helping their children pack for university or plan their weddings. Even my younger cousin, who once borrowed my shoes and raided my closet like a little sister, had a toddler clinging to her hip. And then there I was—childless, partnerless, and trying hard not to feel "less than."

I definitely had my routines. My books. My work as a philosophy professor. I also had my small church community. I had meaningful things to do, but in the quiet moments, it didn't always feel like enough. Some evenings, especially during the winter, loneliness would sneak in like a draft under the door, uninvited but impossible to ignore.

And every time I called my mama, she'd ask gently, "Have you found the man of your dreams yet, baby?"

Her question irked me because she seemed to compare me to everyone else in her life, especially her friends.

I'd laugh and say, "No, Mama, not yet." My voice always tried to sound casual, but, deep down, it stung. Not necessarily because she was pressuring me—Mama never did that—but because her question reminded me of what I hadn't found.

She'd always follow with, "He's out there, honey. And when you meet him, you'll just know. You'll feel it in your bones."

It sounded like something from a novel, sweet yet unrealistic for me. I wasn't naïve. I knew that if the right person was out there, I would eventually find him. But when exactly would this happen? I was becoming impatient, but I wasn't bitter. I had simply made peace with the possibility that love might never be mine.

Then, one snowy Saturday afternoon, I curled into my lounger by the window with the local newspaper in hand, which was my usual ritual. I skimmed all the headlines, as I usually did, and sighed at the state of the world. Then I read the Arts section twice. But when I flipped to the classifieds, usually an afterthought, I paused.

There it was: the Connections section. A dozen little ads written by people who were looking for companionship. One was a retired widower looking for a walking partner. Another, a woman seeking a kind soul who loved jazz. Each blurb was short, hopeful, and even raw in its own way. None of them felt desperate—just open and even brave. They seemed to have so much courage to announce to the world that they were looking for love and companionship.

And I thought, *If they can be brave, why can't I?*

Before I had time to second-guess myself, I grabbed a pen and notepad. I scribbled a few lines, crumpled the paper, and then started again. I wanted to be honest without sounding as if I were placing an order for a soulmate. Yet that was precisely what I was doing.

I wrote something like this:

> *Kindhearted, thoughtful woman, 40, instructor, loves books, quiet mornings and evenings, and deep conversations. Faith is important to me. Looking to meet someone who values integrity, gentleness, and laughter. Open to friendship, possibly more.*

I mailed it before the post office closed that afternoon. As I slipped the envelope into the mailbox, my heart thumped as if I'd just jumped off a cliff. I had no idea why I had such a reaction at the time. But there was no denying it. It felt really different—something I'd never felt before then.

A week passed. Then another. I didn't expect much. I told myself I'd done something brave, and that was enough. But then, in the second week of February, a cream-colored envelope arrived in my mailbox.

Inside was a letter, handwritten in careful script. It began:

Dear kindhearted instructor,

I read your ad and felt compelled to respond. Your words spoke to me—quietly, gently, in a way I didn't expect. My name is Jim. I'm a high school English teacher here in Stratford. I also live with my mother, who's in her 80s and needs some care. I'm a reader, a walker, a lover of words and music. I believe in God, in slow mornings and evenings, and in the beauty of stillness. If you're open to corresponding, I'd love to hear from you.

I must have read the letter ten times that night. There was something so genuine, so reassuring about it. No fluff. No gimmicks. He just seemed like a man telling his story and inviting me to share mine.

We began writing weekly. The anticipation of his letters became a quiet joy. His writing was full of insight and humor. He told me about growing up in Stratford, how he'd lost his father recently, how he'd once dreamed of becoming an actor but found a different calling in teaching English and drama. I told him about my love of literature, how I wrote poetry when no one was looking.

Also, I mentioned to him how my heart ached for companionship even though I rarely admitted it.

After a few letters, he included his home number and invited me to call. I hesitated at first. But something inside me propelled me forward.

I waited three days before I called him. My hands were shaking. I was hoping I wouldn't be all choked up.

His phone rang three times before I heard his warm baritone "Hello?"

Our first conversation lasted two hours. We talked about teaching, about our students, about the books that shaped us. He asked thoughtful questions. He laughed easily. He listened without interrupting, a skill I hadn't realized I missed as much as I did. It seemed to be as natural as breathing for him. But, more than that, I felt comfortable while speaking to him. I told him so much about myself, and he shared similar stories about his own life.

We began speaking every other night. There were no cell phones back then—just landlines—so we'd plan our calls like appointments. I'd sit by the phone with a cup of chamomile tea, heart fluttering each time it rang. And each time we spoke for hours.

By the end of the month, we had agreed to meet in person. Sunday brunch at the Queen's Inn. A neutral, cozy place with good coffee and even better pancakes.

I arrived early, nerves twisting my stomach. I wore my favorite navy coat and a soft scarf my friend had knitted for me a while ago. It always made me feel beautiful and confident. I had no idea what to expect. But I was nervous.

Then he walked in. I felt the air change in the room. He was tall and had a gentle smile, his coat dusted with snow. He spotted me and waved a little awkwardly, endearingly so. When we shook hands, there was something in the warmth of his grasp that calmed me.

We talked through brunch. And lunch. And nearly until afternoon tea. There were no awkward pauses, no moments of scrambling for conversation. We shared stories. We laughed. Interestingly, we discovered we went to the same church but had never seen each other, something that now feels impossible. He told me about his mother, a strong-willed woman who still baked bread every Sunday. I told him about my mama, who still hoped I'd find love.

What struck me most was not just what he said, but how he listened. He gave me his full attention, not just with his ears. He even let the silence linger when needed. There was no rush and no need to impress anyone. There was just genuine conversation and sharing. I had never experienced that before.

We began seeing each other regularly after that. We took walks along the Avon River weekly. Sunday Mass was usually followed by brunch at the Queen's Inn. We also had bookstore dates where we would go from one bookstore to another, either in London or Kitchener. He brought me fresh scones from his mother's favorite bakery. I brought him novels I thought he'd enjoy.

Over time, I met his mother. She was a stern woman with a kind heart, who reminded me of a retired general in an apron. She was wary at first, but one afternoon, after I helped her frost a cake, she leaned in and whispered, "I'm glad he found you."

Jim and I dated for about a year. It was a year of slow growth, of learning more about each other's rhythms, and of sharing more and more about ourselves. We also shared tears and laughter. He held me when I cried about a difficult day at the university. I held his hand when his mother had a health scare.

One spring evening, as cherry blossoms bloomed around us, he said, "I know this might sound sudden, but I've known since our first brunch that I want to build a life with you."

I nodded, tears in my eyes. "Me too."

We married the following fall in a simple church ceremony. My mama wore a lavender dress and cried the entire time. Jim's mother sat proudly in the front row, dabbing her eyes with a lace handkerchief. It was a moment that I will never forget.

Now, after almost twenty-five years together, I still marvel at how things unfolded as they did. How, one lonely winter day, my life changed in a heartbeat. A newspaper ad. A handwritten letter. It could so easily have been missed. But we found each other.

I believe now, more than ever, that love is not something we earn. It is not a prize for patience or good behavior. It is a gift. A divine one. And we never know how God will bless us in our lives and how He will answer our prayers.

I always prayed that I would meet a man who shared my values and passions. I also hoped that my husband would share my faith and enjoy going to church with me. But I knew that my latter request was definitely in the hands of the Almighty.

It's hard to believe how our lives can be blessed beyond words when we least expect them to be. We just have to have faith and believe. This whole process made me realize that I am not really in charge of my life. But God is.

We could pray and ask for what we'd like. But only God will provide in His own time and in His own way. We have no control over whether He will provide or how He will answer our prayers. We just have to truly believe in God's providence. And that's the hard part, especially if we feel desperate to make things happen.

And, sometimes, when I look at Jim reading on the couch beside me, his glasses slipping down his nose, or when he takes my hand as we walk into church, I whisper to myself, *"Who would have thought?"*

But then I smile.

Because God did.

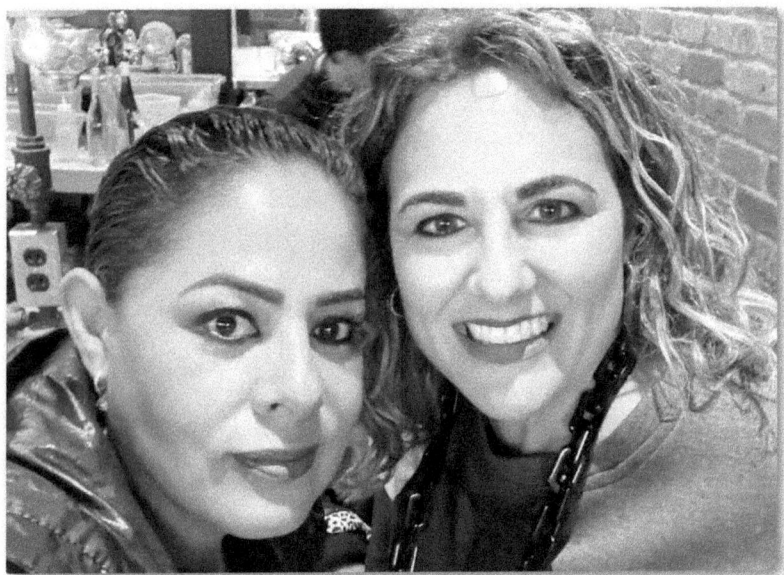

Rafaela and Lisa

A Love Story in Two Languages

Lisa Michelle Umina

They say love knows no boundaries,
and I believe that, because I crossed an airport,
a language, a fear, and an entire country to find mine.

When I landed at Chicago O'Hare International Airport, a chauffeur stood waiting for me with a sign that read, "Lisa Umina, Author." In that moment, I felt something shift. I was officially being recognized as an author for the very first time. It felt magical.

As I made my way to the Latino Book Fair, I couldn't stop smiling. The idea that such an event existed, a celebration of literature attended by hundreds of fellow

Latinos—filled me with joy and a sense of belonging I hadn't expected. Still, I was nervous. My children's book had been translated into Spanish, but I didn't speak Spanish, and I wondered how I would manage. But, as always, a little faith and resourcefulness came through, especially in the form of a table generously stacked with hundreds of Spanish-English dictionaries. Gracias to whoever thought of that!

I was getting settled, snapping photos of my author table and with fellow authors, signing a few books in advance. I always like to add a little drawing of Milo in each book; it's my signature touch. My stomach fluttered with nerves as the doors opened, and the crowd began streaming into the fair.

A kind woman nearby noticed me fussing with my display and offered to help. She showed me how to stack my books in a way that would catch children's eyes, and it worked. Grateful for her warmth, I listened as she encouraged me to go meet the other authors at the event. I reminded her that my Spanish was limited. She simply smiled and said, "I'll translate for you."

We made our way to Dr. Abel Cruz's table, an impressive display overflowing with the many books he had authored. His presence was magnetic, the kind that commands quiet respect without needing to say a word. But just as I was taking it all in, something—or rather *someone*—shifted my focus entirely. Standing beside him was a beautiful woman, poised, radiant, and unforgettable.

When we were introduced, she looked at me with calm confidence and asked, "Do you speak Spanish?"

I smiled and replied, "No."

She nodded softly and said simply, "Nice to meet you," then turned away. There was a touch of sarcasm in her tone, but just as quickly, she turned back laughing and began talking to me. It was an unassuming exchange. A moment you might miss if you weren't paying attention. But something in the way she said those words stayed with me. That phrase *"mucho gusto,"* in both English and Spanish, would come to carry a depth and meaning neither of us could have imagined in that moment.

Her name was Rafaela. And one day, she would become my wife. If I could've seen the future that day, could've seen how deeply our love would be tested, I might've held her hand a little tighter.

***

Years passed full of laughter, everyday joys, and quiet moments that stitched our lives together. But then came the test we never expected. After numerous screenings, biopsies, and cautious optimism, this time, the results weren't in her favor. I had never seen her in that light before, vulnerable in the face of something so out of our control. I expected to be devastated. And truthfully, I was. The word *cancer* hit like a punch to the chest. But what caught me off guard wasn't the diagnosis; it was her response.

She didn't collapse under the weight of it. I'm not saying she didn't feel every ounce of fear, sadness, or anger—of course, she did. But somehow, what she radiated most was determination. She had one focus: to get through it. To beat it. And she did.

Watching her fight was unlike anything I'd ever experienced. This was the person who had always been the light in my life, the best part of my soul, and now she was suffering. With every chemo session, every appointment, every sleepless night, I stayed hopeful. Not because I was in denial, but because I refused to give my energy to any other outcome.

She wasn't going to go through this alone. Not for a single moment. And today, after all the battles she's fought, she stands here with her breast cancer in remission, a survivor in every sense of the word.

***

That night in Chicago, we went out for drinks, and I swear I could hear my heart beating louder than the music. I was nervous, not because of the cocktails or the city lights, but because I was about to confess something huge. I wanted to tell Rafaela that I had feelings for her. I also wanted to tell her…I was gay. You know, just a casual little conversation over drinks.

Back then, coming out wasn't something you just did, especially not at a professional event like a book fair, and certainly not as an author known for writing books about God. The stakes felt even higher. I worried how people would reconcile my faith with my truth, and whether there would still be space for me in the literary world I was beginning to call home. There was a quiet, persistent fear that followed me: fear of being judged, of losing opportunities, of being seen differently. If I said the wrong thing, I risked everything. I might not be invited back, my work might be dismissed, or worse…what if Rafaela wasn't gay? I wasn't just putting my heart on the line; I was risking a connection that had already become important to me. The thought of losing that scared me more than I wanted to admit.

But something deep inside me knew I had to say it. I had never felt anything like this before, the immediate, unshakable connection. Who meets someone and, within twenty-four hours, thinks, *This could be the person I've been waiting for*? It defied logic, but it felt undeniably real. There was a quiet certainty in my heart, the kind that doesn't ask for permission or explanation. But then, logic tried to barge in—*She's from Mexico; I'm from the US… How the heck are we going to make this work? Long-distance dating from two different countries?*

I gave it a solid thirty seconds of thought. Maybe fifteen. Honestly, if I was brave enough to tell someone I had feelings for them, I figured we could sort the rest out later. So I went for it. And by "went for it," I mean I basically shouted it over the bar noise as if I were ordering a drink. "I'M GAY!" I half expected the music to screech to a halt like in the movies. All eyes on me. Bartender dropping a glass. Dramatic pause.

But none of that happened. Instead, Rafaela smiled, leaned in, and simply said, "Me too."

Well, we did it; we started dating. We traveled together across the US, meeting in different cities for book fairs and carving out a love story between airports and hotel lobbies. I started learning Spanish, but she picked up English even faster. Somehow, we always found a way to understand each other, even when the words weren't perfect.

Our last book fair together was in California, and we ended the trip with a magical day at Disneyland. That day felt different. I had known for a while, maybe even a year, that we were reaching a turning point. It was time to make a real decision about our future, something bigger than flights and weekend trips.

The day I returned home, I went straight to my counselor. I told her I was thinking about visiting Rafaela in Mexico, not just for a trip, but to explore the possibility of building a life there. She nodded, smiled, and said, "That sounds like a beautiful next step."

I agreed. In fact, I agreed so wholeheartedly that I walked straight to the car, called my friend, and said, "Book my flight. I'm going tomorrow to Mexico at 4:00 a.m."

What moved me most about that trip, what still stays with me, was how Rafaela made space for me in her world with barely twenty-four hours' notice. Somehow, in that short window, she carved out a week that felt like a lifetime. She took me to some of the most beautiful places in Mexico, places full of color, history, and soul. We shared unforgettable meals, laughed over street tacos and dinners, and found a rhythm that already felt like home.

But the moment that truly touched my heart was when we drove nearly two hours out of the city to her hometown of Santiago. It was there, surrounded by her family, that something clicked. The warmth in the room, the smell of a lovingly prepared meal, the joyful chaos of nieces and nephews dancing and laughing, it felt as if I was being folded into something sacred. A life. A family. A future.

By the time I boarded my flight back to Cleveland, there was no doubt in my mind. I was ready to pack up my life and start a new one. As hard as it would be to say goodbye to my own family, I knew in my heart I wasn't losing one; I was gaining another. And in Mexico, love was already waiting for me.

It felt surreal when I boarded the airplane to return to Mexico. I had sold my house, said goodbye to my family, and there I was, thousands of feet in the air, headed to a new country, new experiences, and a new language. And honestly, I was more excited than scared.

Looking back now, I think, *Wow...I probably could've planned that a little better.* But even so, I still would have made the leap.

One of the hardest parts about starting life in Mexico was the language. I had to learn Spanish from scratch. As I worked on that, I was also figuring out who I was in this new place. I had to completely redefine myself. For the first year, I went everywhere with Rafaela. We were like two teenagers fresh out of high school, young, in love, and wide-eyed about the world. Looking back, we had so many beautiful, unforgettable moments.

One of the biggest challenges for me, though, was adjusting to the culture. Rafa comes from a *big* family; back then, there were about thirty of them, and now it's closer to fifty. The family traditions were strong and deeply rooted. And while they're now one of the things I treasure most about my life here, it took some getting used to.

I remember one Christmas vividly. We were preparing to celebrate in Santiago, and I had no idea what to expect. No one explained the customs, and I just tried to go with the flow. It was two in the afternoon; we'd grabbed a pizza, checked into a hotel, and everything seemed normal. I thought we'd have dinner in a few hours, maybe relax.

At around five, I started sipping some wine. Then six o'clock passed. Seven. Still no dinner. I was getting tipsy and a little confused. Turns out, we weren't eating until *midnight*. And even then, it wasn't dinner that kicked off the celebration.

At the stroke of midnight, everyone began passing around baby Jesus figurines while singing a song to celebrate the birth of Christ. I was totally caught off guard and, admittedly, more than a little buzzed. I didn't know the tradition and was embarrassed. Where I come from, Christmas morning starts *in the morning*. You make coffee, eat some cookies, open gifts, and listen to Barbra Streisand's Christmas album. That definitely wasn't happening here. Not that year. We didn't get back to the hotel until four in the morning.

But we both learned something from that night. Now, it's one of our funniest memories. Not so much in the moment, but definitely in hindsight.

On the way back to the city, neither of us spoke for the entire two-hour drive. The silence was thick, but not unfamiliar; we were both still simmering from the argument. When we finally got back to the house, I made an offhand comment that I had absolutely no desire to make a rack of lamb for her. Without missing a beat, she told me to shove that rack of lamb somewhere it definitely didn't belong.

I remember walking into the bedroom, shutting the door behind me, and just bursting out laughing. I thought, *Gosh, even when we fight, she's still so adorable.* And honestly, that hasn't changed. We've had our fair share of intense moments, but we've never crossed the line into disrespect. That's something I really value about our relationship.

One of the hardest parts, though, is navigating a multiracial relationship where two different cultures are constantly at play. Sometimes things just don't align; what makes sense in one culture can feel completely off in the other. A lot of our arguments over the years haven't even been about big issues; they were simply the result of miscommunication. The language barriers, the different ways we express things, it can all lead to confusion over what we *meant* versus what was *actually said.* But at the end of the day, we've learned how to laugh through it, love through it, and keep growing together.

The next big move wasn't geographical—it was internal. It was learning to truly believe in myself again. Back in the US, I had built something I was incredibly proud of: *The Milo and Lisa Show,* a dynamic school program in which I performed using eleven different voices and sound effects; it reached nearly 5,000 students a week. I was living my purpose, sharing stories, inspiring kids, and feeling deeply connected to my craft.

But when I moved to Mexico, everything came to a halt. I couldn't speak the language, and I was no longer able to visit schools. Suddenly, my platform disappeared, and I found myself in unfamiliar territory, not just geographically, but emotionally. So I took a one-year pause. And honestly, I'm grateful I did. That time allowed me to be present—with Rafaela, with her family, and with myself. I spent time at their office, got to know her world, and finally gave myself permission to just *be*. After all, I had been working since I was twelve. Coming to Mexico at thirty-five wasn't just a new chapter, it was a whole new book.

I decided to start at home. I remember the day Rafaela surprised me by transforming a spare room into a beautiful home office. She bought me a desk, a shelf, a computer—everything I needed to begin again. And still, I had no idea what I was going to do.

Then, one day, someone asked me for a consultation. Just like that, a door cracked open. One opportunity led to another. Fast-forward to today, and I own two international publishing companies. And through it all, Rafaela has been right there beside me.

I'll never forget the day I told her I wanted an office outside the house. She looked at me and said, "I'm not ready for that."

I asked her, "What would it take?"

She replied, "At least ten authors." Challenge accepted. And when I hit ten, she was already out scouting locations. That's the kind of woman she is—measured, loyal, and quietly brilliant.

Every major step I've taken, she's been there—steady, supportive, and invested. And I've been there for her, too, through so many milestones and life changes. Looking back now, I don't believe anyone truly succeeds alone. You must be willing to ask for help. You have to let people in.

And even now, more than two decades later, I can say without hesitation that the woman sitting across from me at any dinner table, or in any moment of my life, is still the best part of me. We're celebrating our twenty-first anniversary this year. Last year, we marked our twentieth by traveling to Europe, visiting different places, and celebrating with friends and family who've been part of our journey. Looking back now, part of me still can't believe it's been twenty-one years. And yet, another part of me absolutely can.

We've lived through so much together, every twist life could offer. We've said goodbye to loved ones: our fathers, John and Abel and Rafaela's mother, Kilita. We've faced illness and recovery, heartbreak and healing, and just…life in all its unpredictable, beautiful mess.

As we grow older, we begin to see more clearly what truly matters. The things we once thought were so important fade into the background. What remains is love, loyalty, and the quiet strength of showing up, again and again, for one another.

To still be here, side by side, with the hope and intention of celebrating twenty-one more years together is nothing short of extraordinary. It's a triumph over every storm we've weathered, a testament to love's resilience. And as we look ahead, I carry a deep gratitude for every sunrise we greet together, knowing that our story, against all odds —is still being written.

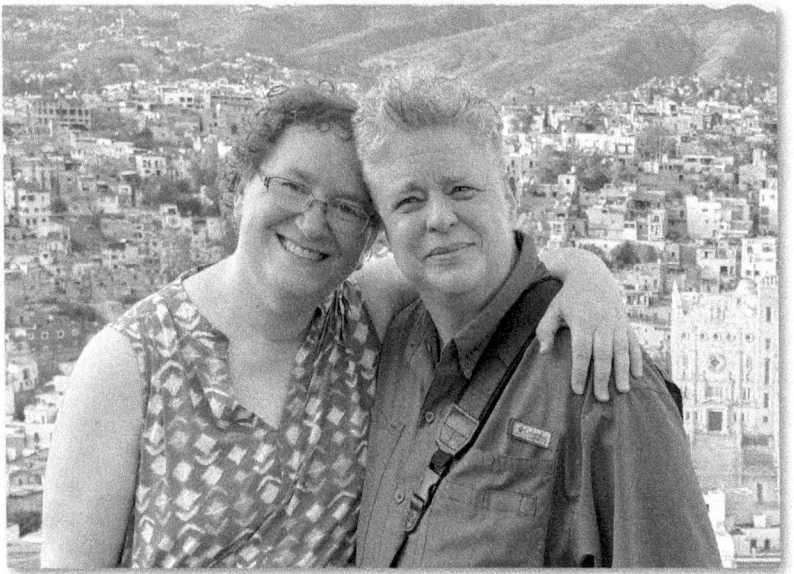

Bethany and Kit

A Queer Journey Home

Bethany Zare

L ove doesn't always come in the form we expect. Queer love, in its fluid and expansive form, offered me something I never knew I needed, a journey home.

"A Queer Journey Home" is not just a love story; it's a story about becoming, healing, and redefining chosen identity. This is a midlife romance anchored on finding safety and trust after trauma, shaped by healing gender transformations and allowing my partner to help me redefine desire.

This happens to be a queer romance, but its lessons about intimacy, forgiveness, and acceptance are universal.

Too Young to Consent

My first experience with love came from a music teacher. I was fifteen, craving attention, and eager to be seen. A much older man made me feel like the "chosen one." At the time, he praised my horn playing, said I was special. I clung to those words despite the blurring of boundaries and the inappropriate affection.

I wanted to announce our love from the mountaintops but was told to keep it a secret. This suppressed my expression of passion. I learned early on that I didn't get a voice in the relationship and that silence was the cost of being together. Looking back now, I see clearly what I couldn't name then—I never truly had the ability to consent.

As I grew into a young woman, I started to feel doubt about my choices, especially around men. I internalized being an object more than a person, my value assessed only through the lens of desire, not based on my worth. I stopped trusting not only men but myself. I avoided being seen as feminine. Anything soft, expressive, or beautiful felt like a liability that would invite the wrong kind of attention. I buried my vulnerable parts. Being seen as a woman felt risky, and I didn't have the tools to keep myself safe.

I chose a career in music to heal that rupture of trust. Much later in life, I was able to make peace with my past. The shame I was carrying didn't belong to me. I honor the love my younger self experienced, despite its challenges.

It was one of my first experiences with love, and it had a lasting impact into my adulthood.

Coming Out

Everyone's journey with sexuality and identity is different, but for me, something about the straight, heteronormative script never quite fit. I never desired getting married or having kids. I couldn't relate to my friends who dreamed of finding the perfect man.

College exposed me to a kind of diversity I'd never encountered before, not just in backgrounds or identities, but in ways of thinking, living, and loving. For the first time, I met people who existed outside the boxes I had thought to be the norm. There were students who had relationships that didn't follow the typical script. I met women who were loud and unapologetic; others moved quietly but with deep self-assurance. Being around them stirred something in me—not just admiration, but possibility. It made me question my own belief system and how I envisioned my life. Slowly, I began to unearth parts of myself that I had buried and never given a chance to shine. I was ready to explore my own freedom.

At twenty-one, I had my first relationship with a woman. I didn't feel as if it was a response to my trauma with men, but it was the first time I felt seen in a way that didn't come with strings attached. Our relationship wasn't perfect, we were both young and trying to find ourselves, but it gave me the safety and tenderness I hadn't felt before. It allowed me to lower the shields—ones I didn't know I had been holding up for years—to allow for real connection.

Throughout the years, I had relationships with both men and women. To me, it's the person who matters, not the body they are packaged in. It is one thing to fall "in lust" with someone, but lasting relationships are built on connections with more than the body.

A Lasting Love

I met Kit on a dating website when I was forty-three. Here was someone who could create a profile using complex compound sentences and didn't need the spell-check button. We were two grown women with enough baggage to fill an airplane, but also enough humor to unpack it together. When Kit arrived at our first date in her dark-blue convertible, I knew she was the one.

We built a life rooted in shared values and a deep love of animals. In 2014, we married, even though I had long believed a certificate was unnecessary to prove our love, and for much of my adult life, the law denied us that right.

Same-sex marriage had been a legal battleground in California for years. It was briefly legal in 2008, before voters passed Proposition 8, banning it again. For five long years, same-sex couples were left in legal limbo. It wasn't until June 2013, when the Supreme Court declined to rule on Prop 8 in *Hollingsworth v. Perry*, that same-sex marriage resumed statewide, and only in 2015, after our marriage, with the case of *Obergefell v. Hodges*, it became a legal right across the United States.

On our wedding day, marrying Kit felt monumental. In a world that had spent decades trying to erase, criminalize, or silence our union, simply standing together and declaring ourselves a family felt revolutionary. It also signified I had conquered my fear of committing to one long-term partner. I never realized how supportive and justifying it would be to use the title Married. It wasn't about a piece of paper. Now, saying "wife" had legal and political implications.

Public displays of affection were rebellious acts. Every kiss between us was our refusal to disappear. We had spent too many years hiding to make others feel more comfortable. Choosing visibility felt as if we were reclaiming what had been denied for so long. It was a way to honor those who had fought, marched, and risked their lives simply so we could have the radical freedom to love openly.

Being together felt as though we were coming home to heal ourselves.

Unseen Scars

Kit and I weathered cancer, depression, and addiction, but still found joy in our married union. Trauma casts a long shadow, and beneath the surface, something was shifting for both of us. I loved Kit deeply, but old, persistent fears lived inside me unresolved. I finally felt safe enough to test the boundaries of what it meant to be us. I had held on to queer identity as a way to reclaim my control and move away from the masculinity that had so powerfully shaped my sexuality.

At first, the doubts came softly, hidden in moonlit reflections or the self-analysis of therapy sessions. What if I had grown up feeling safe in my body, unviolated and unafraid? What if I had trusted men? Could I have loved a man or even married one? These questions were too scary to speak aloud. They felt like betrayals, not only to Kit, but to the queer community and to me. I began to wonder if I would ever be healed "enough."

Simultaneously, I could feel Kit pulling away, as we both filled our days independently and became less and less connected. We didn't stop loving each other, but we no longer knew how to speak each other's language. Kit's outlook on life was so different from mine that I started to question who I had become. The harm done to me by a man had distorted the lens through which I saw everything, including intimacy. I was only just beginning to realize how deeply the past had rooted itself in my life.

Shape-Shifting Love

As if on cue, Kit was having their own doubts about, not only our relationship, but their own identity. At the age fifty-five, Kit came out as trans. Kit changed their pronouns to *he/him* and started wearing men's clothes, nice clothes. Suddenly, he cared how he looked and no longer dressed in oversized T-shirts and baggy jeans; he was no longer too depressed to get out of bed, no longer unable to look in the mirror. Kit was finally feeling truly himself.

At first, I was afraid I would lose everything: my wife, my identity as a queer person, and the life we had carefully built. It turns out, however, that Kit's transition was not a rupture but a revelation.

Through his eyes, I witnessed masculinity reconstructed —a sensitive male, somebody who felt safe to me, somebody who wasn't going to threaten or hurt me, and somebody who was able to express himself. Most men aren't allowed to show their feelings. They need to show up big, bold, powerful, and strong. This doesn't leave a lot of room for sensitivity and nuance.

Kit had the ability to live as a man after experiencing life in a woman's body. He showed me that masculinity could coexist with tenderness, softness, even sacred vulnerability. Many trans men have spent much time contemplating and thinking about what masculinity means and how they want to show up in the world.

Kit hadn't changed his essence. He had grown deeper into himself. Loving him through his gender-defining transition invited me to do the same. I, too, was able to lean into becoming more female. I bought a dress for the first time since childhood. I realized my queerness had never been about excluding men; rather, it was about escaping harm. And when masculinity was stripped of its violence, I could finally meet it with curiosity and love.

Kit had become the man I never knew I was seeking.

Transformation of Self

This story may be unique in its specifics, but it lives, in conversation with every story in this anthology, as a testament of how love and identity don't stand still. Our ever-shifting, expansive selves flow when we follow the current of our truths. This is not just about of queer love, but of how staying true to oneself means allowing love to change form without losing its depth.

This love story is a radical embrace of living without constraint, healing old stories about gender, and loving beyond boundaries. Love isn't about categories. It is about finding the best versions of ourselves through the eyes of our partners and loving whom we love, even as they, and we, change. When we remember that truth, we make space for love to continue and grow...even into something we didn't plan for.

If you've never walked through a transition like this, you might wonder how it's possible. The truth is *all* love evolves. All long-term relationships carry us through transformation. They ask us to let go of past concepts, to morph and adapt, as we grow alongside another soul and bear witness, as we become more fully ourselves.

Loving Kit taught me that masculinity doesn't have to harm. That healing doesn't require forgetting. Instead, learning how to live with the past opens the door to the future.

I am still queer. I am still healing. I am still learning, every day, how to love myself and others more honestly.

I offer this story not as a political view, but as an example of hope and belonging. While it may seem complicated, it is beautifully simple:

> *Two people fell in love. They both changed.*
> *And love, in its own way, endured.*

This story is a thread in our collective, for queer and straight readers, between whom we once were and who we are becoming. It is about the love we've known and the love that waits to be discovered.

About the Authors

Roberto Alfaro was born in New York City and raised in the South Bronx, where he lived for twenty-four years before moving to Connecticut to become a Hartford police officer in 1979. He retired in 2000 after twenty-one years of dedicated service in the patrol division, on the recruitment team, in the mounted unit, and as a plainclothes officer. In 2021, he also retired from Quinnipiac University as a public safety officer. Today, Roberto continues to enjoy his retirement by working as a professional model, actor, salsa dancer and instructor, motivational speaker, inventor, writer, and author of several books! He currently resides in Hamden, Connecticut, with his beautiful wife and four children.

Renato Bettio (Dr. Roberto Arévalo Araujo MD, FACP) was born in El Salvador. After finishing high school, he traveled to Mexico to continue studying and graduated as a doctor and a surgeon from UNAM in 1970. He then worked at the Oakwood Hospital (Dearborn, Michigan) and at CMDNJ in New Jersey. There he also studied hematology and oncology as a subspecialty. He is board certified in internal medicine, as well as in hematology and oncology. He is the founder of the Cancer and Hematology Center at Pasco County, Florida, a center that offers radiotherapy, immunotherapy, and chemotherapy. He is also a founder of the Medical Mission of Mercy / Medical Mission International, whose goal it is to take free medical, surgical, and ophthalmologic treatment to homeless people east of El Salvador. This mission has been recognized by the Congress of El Salvador and was nominated for a Nobel Prize.

Donna Bond, MA, is a former Ritz-Carlton marketing executive who walked away from corporate success to answer the deeper call of her soul. Today, she is a Soul Catalyst, Spiritual Psychology Coach, and founder of Consciousness Rising, Inc., dedicated to guiding spiritually awakening women back to the truth of who they are.

She is the author of *Original Wisdom: Harness the Power of the Authentic You*, and the creator of the transformational healing modality Higher Human Integration™. As host of the experiential show **Spiritual Ambition**, Donna helps women release who they've been taught to be—so they can embody their sacred soul signature and live in alignment with their higher purpose.

Her work weaves together the deep insight of spiritual psychology, gene keys, and the deep presence, offering a grounded, heart-centered path for soul-aligned living. Donna supports conscious, successful women who are discontent with a life that no longer fits—and are ready to integrate every facet of their lives with the power, presence, and wisdom of their soul.

Her highest mission is soul liberation: awakening the whole self through truth, presence, and divine remembrance.

Learn more at donnabond.com.

Lisa Cassman is an author, speaker, pastor, and life coach. She holds a PhD in clinical pastoral counseling. Residing with her husband, Steve, in Northern Minnesota, together they have raised four boys and are delighted by their twelve grandchildren. Lisa is passionate about seeing people experience God's love and freedom in His precepts. This is her tenth published book after writing titles on marriage, prayer, personal growth, as well as a children's book, a devotional, and a volume of poetry.

Irene Roth is a freelance writer and author. She was born in Montreal, but now lives in Ontario with her husband (Jim), Toby, and Milo. She has a master's degree in philosophy and psychology and uses her expertise in these areas to write books for adults and teens on how to live an excellent life. She enjoys writing self-help books for adults about how to live a good quality of life with chronic illness. She also teaches workshops for Savvy Authors. When she's not teaching and writing, she is actively involved in the Fibro Support Network in the London, Ontario area. She runs workshops on writing and mindset matters, just to name a few. Again, her goal is to encourage and inspire people to live quality lives while managing fibromyalgia.

Lisa Michelle Umina is an award-winning author, publisher, speaker, and podcast host. As the founder and CEO of Halo Publishing International, she has helped bring over 3,000 titles to life since 2002. Lisa is the author of several acclaimed books, including *Milo and the Green Wagon*, *Milo Finds His Best Friend*, *Milo Moments*, and the anthologies *The Journey is the Gift: The Moment that Changed My Story*, *Shattered Silence: Stories of Loss and Healing*, *Lecciones de vida: El momento que cambió mi historia*, and *The Courage to Begin Again: Stories of Resilience, Courage, and Reinvention*. With more than two decades of experience in the publishing industry, she is a passionate mentor to authors around the world, offering expert guidance on writing, marketing, and self-publishing. Lisa also hosts the Award-Winning Authors podcast, where she spotlights powerful voices and shares insights from across the literary landscape.

Her work and collaborations with industry leaders such as Ingram Book Group, the Independent Book Publishers Association (IBPA), and Publishers Weekly have solidified Lisa's reputation as a respected leader in the publishing industry, continually elevating the standards and reach of independent publishing on a global scale.

Bethany Zare is a professional French horn player in Symphony San Jose and the Monterey Symphony, as well as a union officer for the American Federation of Musicians based in San Francisco, California.

After graduating with a bachelor's degree in music performance from the University of Southern California, she spent eight years playing her horn in Mexico. She is married to Kit Zare, a professional photographer. They own two German shepherds and reside in Monterey.

Bethany's first book of poems and art, Pearl's Wisdom, was released in May 2025 and can be found at Halo Publishing.

halopublishing.com/authors/bethany-zare/

Founded in 2002, Halo Publishing International is a hybrid publisher dedicated to helping authors around the world bring their stories to life. We offer flexible and affordable publishing options that blend the best of traditional and self-publishing. Our services include professional editing, custom cover design, formatting, printing, global distribution, and marketing support.

Whether you're writing fiction, nonfiction, children's books, or faith-based works, our mission is to empower you to publish with quality, integrity, and confidence.

Follow us on our social media
HaloPublishingInternational

To know more about Halo Publishing International please visit
www.halopublishing.com

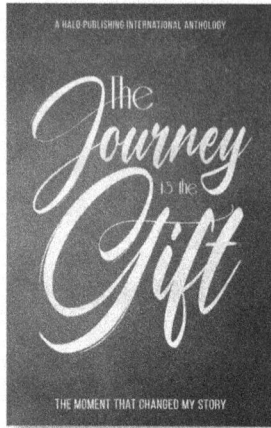

The Journey is the Gift: The Moment that Changed My Story is an anthology of resilience and transformation. Each author confronts life's unexpected challenges—whether accident, addiction, loss, or sudden change—and emerges profoundly altered. These stories reveal how unforeseen trials reshape identity and perspective. More than survival, they embody growth, strength, and renewal. This collection stands as testament to the miracle of living beyond coping, into thriving.

**The Journey is the Gift:
The Moment that Changed My Story**

ISBN Hardcover: 978-1-63765-356-2
ISBN Paperback: 978-1-63765-357-9
Hardcover Price: $21.95
Paperback Price: $18.95
eBook Price: $4.95
Page Count: 126

SHATTERED
SILENCE

Shattered Silence: Stories of Loss and Healing is a poignant collection that explores the profound journey through grief and the transformative power of healing. Through a series of compelling narratives, this book offers a glimpse into the shattered silence that follows loss, and the courageous individuals who navigate the challenging path toward healing.

Shattered Silence:
Stories of Loss and Healing

ISBN Hardcover: 978-1-63765-550-4
ISBN Paperback: 978-1-63765-600-6
Hardcover Price: $21.95
Paperback Price: $18.95
eBook Price: $4.95
Page Count: 198

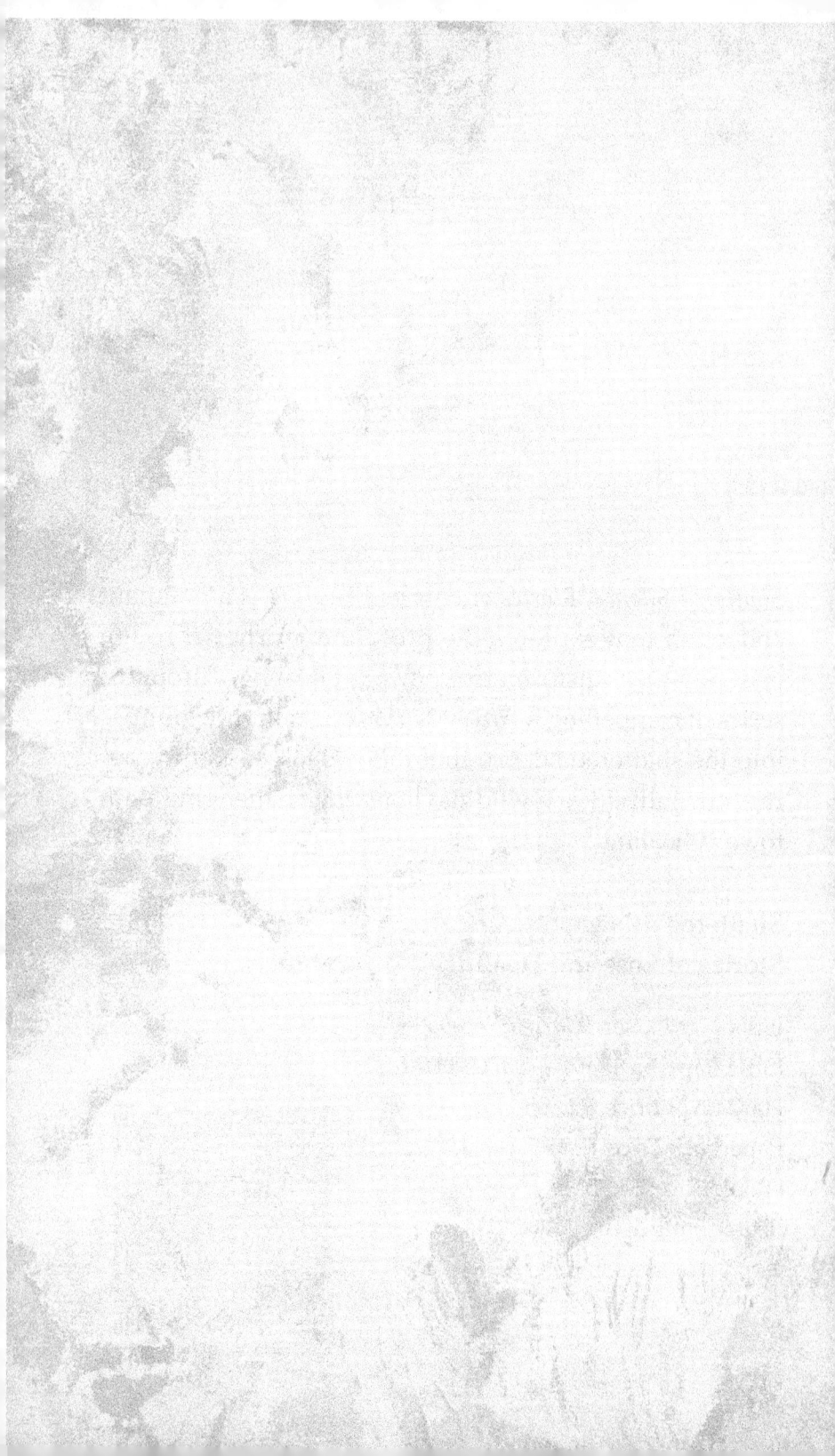

www.ingramcontent.com/pod-product-compliance
Lightning Source LLC
Chambersburg PA
CBHW052119090426
42741CB00009B/1874